illustrated by Inna Anikeeva

85 BRAIN TEASERS

CREATIVE KIDS

Activity Book

CLEVER
Publishing

ROBOT PLAYDATE

Help the robot find its friends. Follow the path of shapes in the same order as the 4 shapes n the top box.

Finish drawing the robots, then color them in.

ROBOT PARTY

Match each item in the box below to the robot it belongs to. Write the item's letter in the space below each robot.

1. _____

2. _____

3. _____

4. _____

5. _____

6. _____

7. _____

8. _____

9. _____

10. _____

11. _____

12. _____

a)   b)   c)   d)   e)   f)   g)   h)   i)   j)   k)   l)

ICE-CREAM CAFÉ

Use your favorite crayons to color in this picture.

SWEET TREATS

Trace each line to find out the flavor of the sweet treats. Then color them in.

Draw a line between the pairs that are the same. Which treats don't have a match?

TEA PARTY

Look carefully at each picture. Can you find
11 differences between them?

TEAPOT AND TEACUP

Draw a line between the teapot and its matching cup.
How many pairs can you find?

Fill in the boxes so that the objects don't repeat going across or up and down.

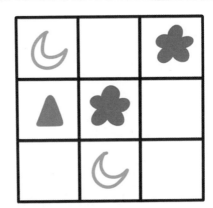

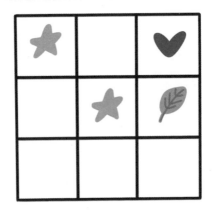

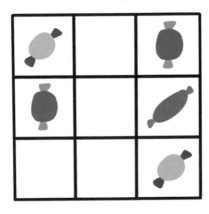

SPACE FLIGHT

Help the cat reach the planet with no one on it.
Be sure to count the stars you pass along the way
and fill in the numbers in the boxes below.

ALIENS

Using the examples below, draw some interesting aliens.
How many body parts did you pick from each list?

	Head	Eyes	Mouth	Body	Hands	Legs	Ears
1							
2							
3							

1

GOING TO THE CIRCUS

Help Pompom find a way through the maze to the ticket booth and then to the circus tent. Don't forget to color in the rest of the tent when you get there!

FINISH

TICKETS

POMPOM

CiRCUS FUN

Can you find three balls that are exactly the same? Circle them, then color in the rest of the picture.

IN THE SKY

Match the helicopters and planes to their shadows below. Then finish coloring the picture.

UP, UP, AND AWAY

Finish drawing the balloons.
Use the squares to guide you.

Trace the dotted lines with a pencil to make a path for each bird to get home.

IN THE YARD

Look carefully at these two pictures. Can you find 16 differences? Circle them when you find them!

IN THE PARK

Bob is looking for his friend at the skate park. Can you help him? His friend is wearing a hat and yellow clothes.

BOB

ROLLER SKATES

Color each skate. If there are parts missing, be sure to add them!

Trace the dotted lines to finish the picture, then color it in. Who do you think will win the race?

IN THE JUNGLE

In this picture, there are 7 monkeys,
1 elephant, and 5 crocodiles. Can you find
them all?

CHAMELEON

This chameleon is hiding! Color the picture by looking at the colored dots. Then see if you can find each of the leaves below in the picture.

BIRTHDAY PARTY

Use your crayons or colored pencils to color in this cheerful birthday party in the woods.

AT THE BEACH

Uh-oh! It looks like some things are mixed up in this picture. Can you find and circle them?

Can you find these small pictures in the big picture?
Which one is NOT in the big picture?

1   2   3   4   5   6

UNDERWATER

Look at the objects in each row. Circle the one that is different from the others.

There are more than 10 fish hiding in the seaweed. Can you find them all? How many are there?

Color in the squares using the key below. What do you see?

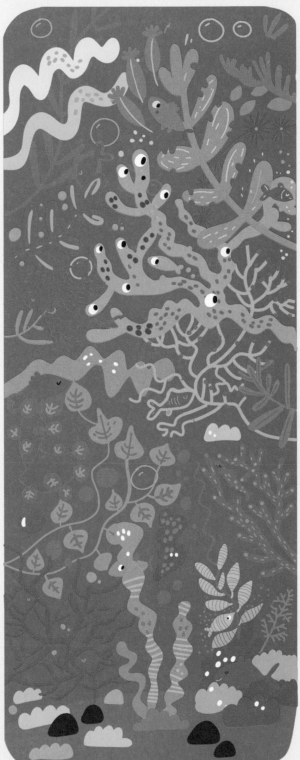

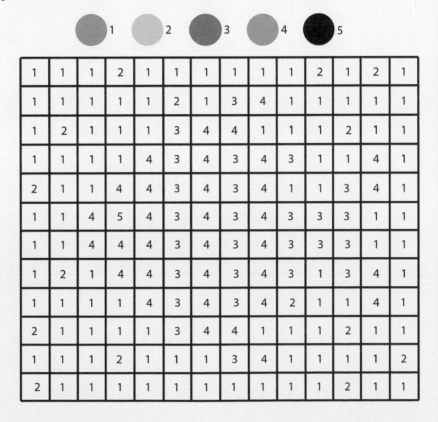

IN THE CITY

Help each character find a path to the place they're looking for. Then color the rest of the picture.

IN THE DESERT

Help the crocodile find a way through the maze to the pyramid. You can only move horizontally or vertically.

FINISH

START

One of these palm trees is different from the rest. Which one is it?

BUILD A BOAT

Look at each picture. Which one has everything needed to build the boat in the center of the page?

Find 10 differences between these two pictures.

IN THE FOREST

This squirrel is gathering food for winter. Can you find the two plates that have the exact same things? Circle them.

COLLECTING

This squirrel is collecting nuts and mushrooms. Can you find a path through the maze to the basket using the directions below?

START

FINISH

4→ 2↓ 5← 2↓ 2→ 1↓ 3→ 1↓

TiME TO EAT!

These two tables look the same, but there is something different between them. Can you find and circle it?

TiME FOR DESSERT!

Use your crayons, markers, or colored pencils to color in the cake, plates, and cups.

IN THE SWAMP

Help the frog find a rare flower. Move according
to the path on the right.

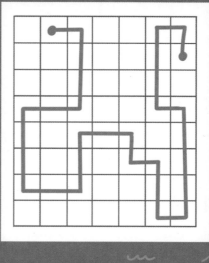

Finish the frogs so that they look the same.

WHAT'S YOUR NAME?

To find out what the frog's name is, follow the thread, but read the letters only on the round beads.

Can you help Frog get to the lake with boats in it?

FROG

FINISH

WHO IS IT?

Starting at the red dot, draw a line by following the directions in the box to the right. The arrows tell you what direction and how many boxes to move. What did you draw?

3↑ 1↘ 1→ 1↘ 2← 1↘ 2← 1↙
3← 2↓ 1↙ 5← 3↗ 2← 1↖
1← 2↖ 1← 1↑ 1→ 1↘ 4→
1↑ 2↖ 4→ 2↘ 1↗ 2→ 1↘

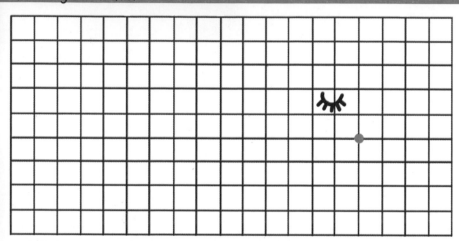

Find the picture using the letter and number clues. Then draw the picture in the box.

	A	B	C	D
1	apple	heart	house	flag
2	caterpillar	flower	star	bow
3	tree	strawberry	rain cloud	leaf
4	mushroom	mug	car	acorn

 2D

 4A

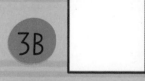 3B

FRONT AND BACK

Look at the photo of the animals taken from the back. Can you find the photo of the same animals, but from the front?

IN THE YARD

Look at the objects in the box. Find and circle them in the big picture, then use your crayons or colored pencils to color the rest of the picture.

TIME FOR A VISIT

Help the cat to go around all the obstacles and get to the big oak tree where his friend lives.

FINISH

IN THE SKY

Look at the boxes below. Match each butterfly to its shadow, color, and antennae shape, and circle it.

Trace the dotted lines with a pencil to guide the butterflies to the flowers.

SEWING STUDIO

Bunny needs certain buttons. Find and circle the buttons that are not red, not green, not round, and have four holes.

Pick the patch that is needed to fix these clothes.

Help the designer finish the dresses: Color the second half, but replace the colors according to the key below. Then color the other dress any way you'd like!

Circle all of the items of clothing.

IN THE MUSEUM

Give Thomas a tour of the museum.
You need to go through all the halls
and then exit the building.

THOMAS

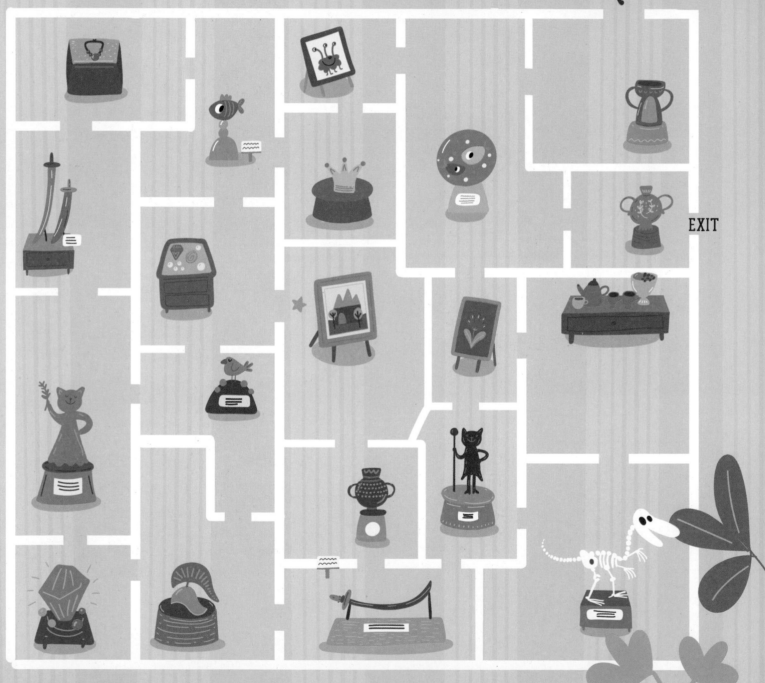

EXIT

IN THE GALLERY

Color the picture according to the key.
What picture do you see?

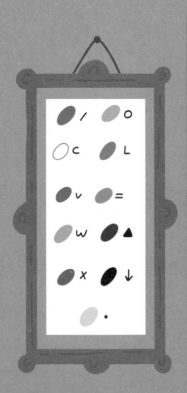

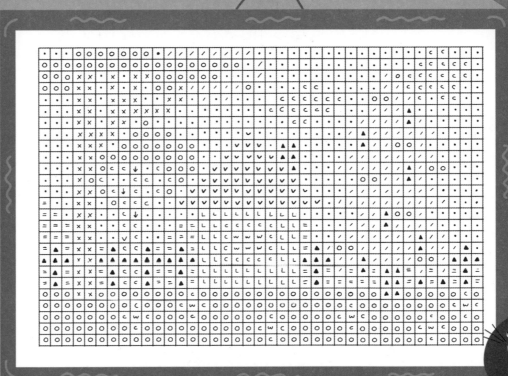

Look at the drawings and copy the pictures in the larger squares.

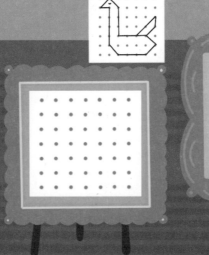

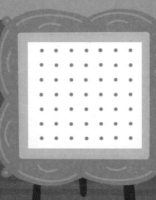

MUSHROOM HOUSE

Color the right half of the mushroom house to match the left half.

MASTER PLAN

Look at this photo of the town. Then find the plan that has all the buildings, trees, and lakes in the same places.

PLANS:

Which bunny shadow is correct?

BIRD PUZZLE

Draw the birds in the grid so that there are different types in the horizontal and vertical rows. Each kind of bird should appear only once in every row and column.

Finish drawing the birds.

BIRD HIDE-AND-SEEK

There are 21 birds hiding in the picture.
Can you find and circle them?

MATCHING GLASSES

Draw ice cubes, fruit, and mint leaves in each glass so that they all are the same.

Find 15 differences between the pictures.

WHAT'S WRONG HERE?

Some things are wrong in this picture. Can you find and circle them?

Fill in the grids so that the objects appear only once in each row and column.

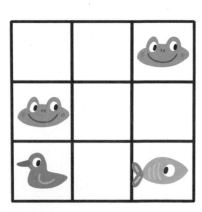

PLAYTIME FUN

There are 20 differences between these two pictures. Find and circle them.

THE BIRDS

IN THE GARDEN

Can you find the small pictures in the bigger picture?

Finish drawing the potted plants using the squares as a guide. Then color the pictures.

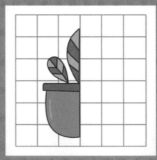

PRETTY PERFUME

Draw flowers in the boxes so that each row and column has the same number of orange and red flowers.

Can you find these flower combinations in the larger picture?

TENT CITY

Read the clues below and see if you can figure out which tent belongs to each animal.
Which tent will remain empty?

My tent is not green and yellow.

There are no patterns on my tent.

I don't like cages or tall tents.

I love pink and polka dots.

My tent is very similar to Bunny's.

Draw a line between the cards that are the same.

BULL'S-EYE!

Follow the lines to see which arrow hit the target in the middle.

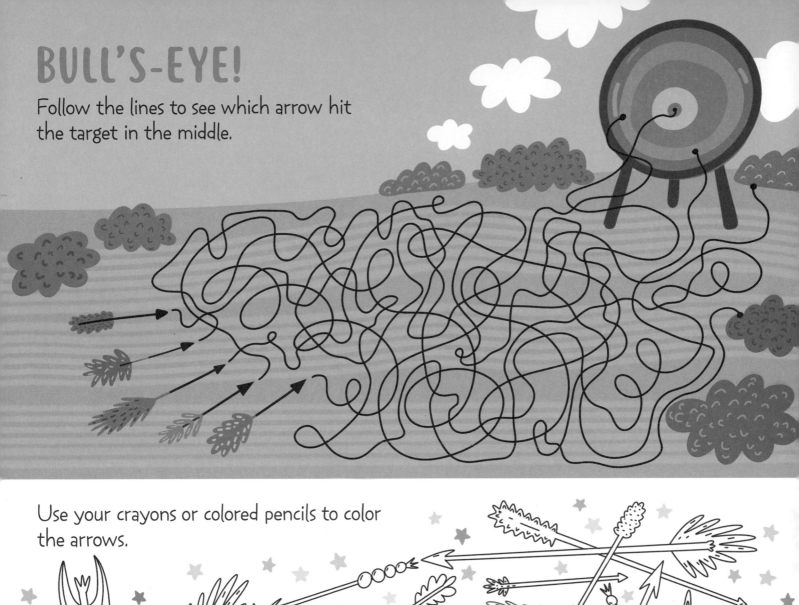

Use your crayons or colored pencils to color the arrows.

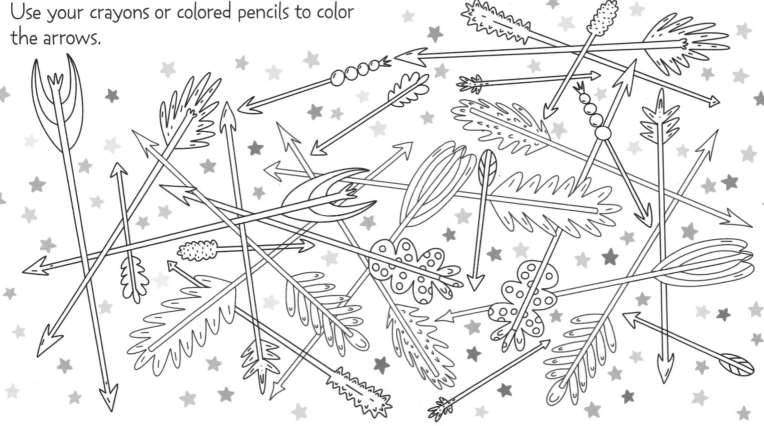

TREASURES

How many of each object do you see?
Write your answers in the boxes below.

Solve the problems using the key above.

1 ⬤   2 ⬡   3 ◈   4 ▮

⬤ + ⬡ =

◈ + ⬤ =

▮ − ⬡ =

⬤ + ▮ =

▮ − ⬤ =

◈ − ⬤ =

◈ + ⬡ =

⬡ + ▮ =

◈ − ◈ =

MATCH THE PATTERN

Look at the pattern to the right. Can you help Bunny find the vase with that same pattern on it?

What does the bear need to open the honey box?

Put a dot in the middle of each box using the code below to find out!

	A	B	C	D	E	F	G
1							
2							
3							
4							
5							
6							
7							
8							
9							

2C, 2D, 3C,
4C, 4D, 2E,
2F, 3F, 4F,
4E, 5E, 6E,
7D, 7E, 8E,
9C, 9D, 9E.

TOWN MATCH

All of the numbered houses are missing the bottom part. Match the correct letter to each number to finish the pictures. Then write the letter in the box next to each number.

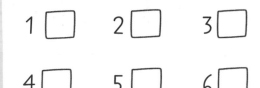

1 ☐ 2 ☐ 3 ☐

4 ☐ 5 ☐ 6 ☐

1

2

3

4

5

6

A

B

C

D

E

F

Draw another house in this space. Use the boxes to help you!

I LOVE ART!

Trace the dotted lines to complete the picture.
Then color it in.

Match each house on the left with
the correct parts on the right.

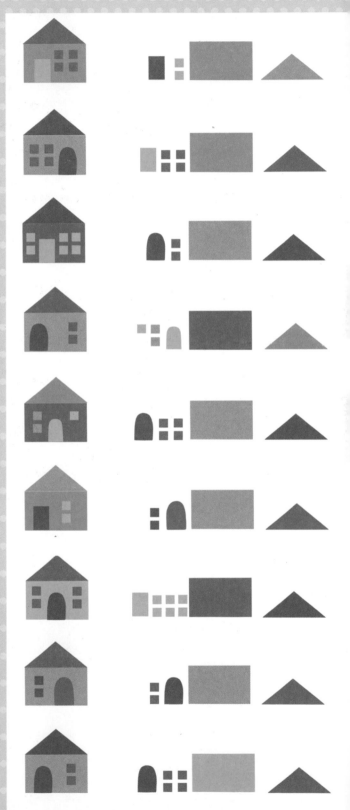

GOING TO THE CiRCUS

Help Mr. Pig find the quickest way to the circus tent.

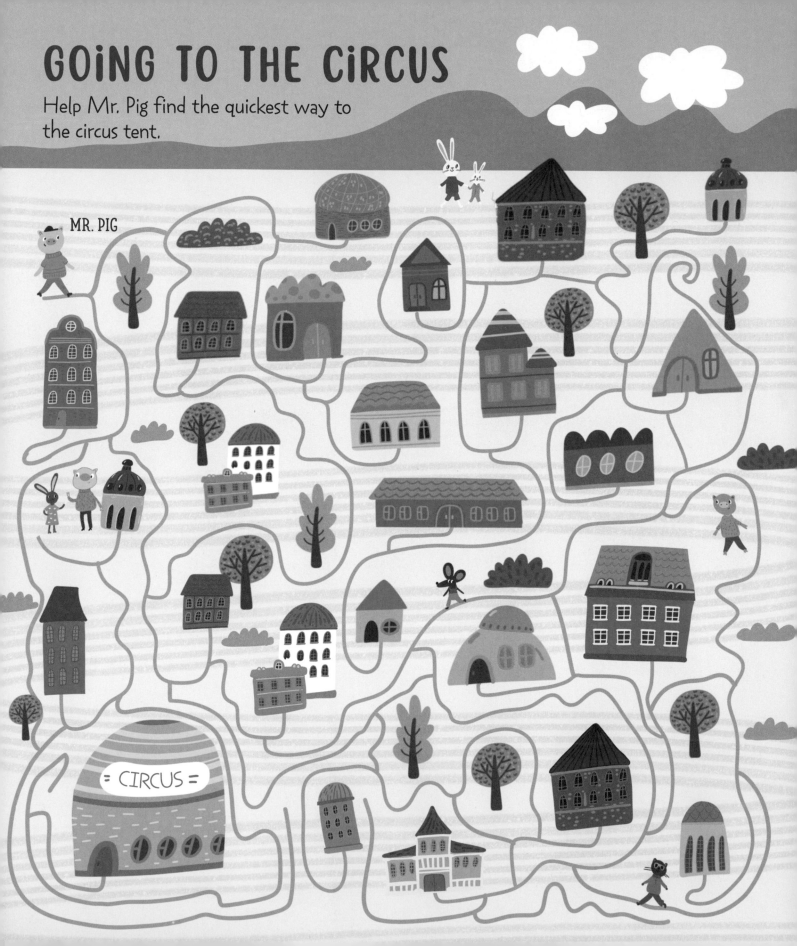

MR. PIG

= CIRCUS =

AT THE CIRCUS

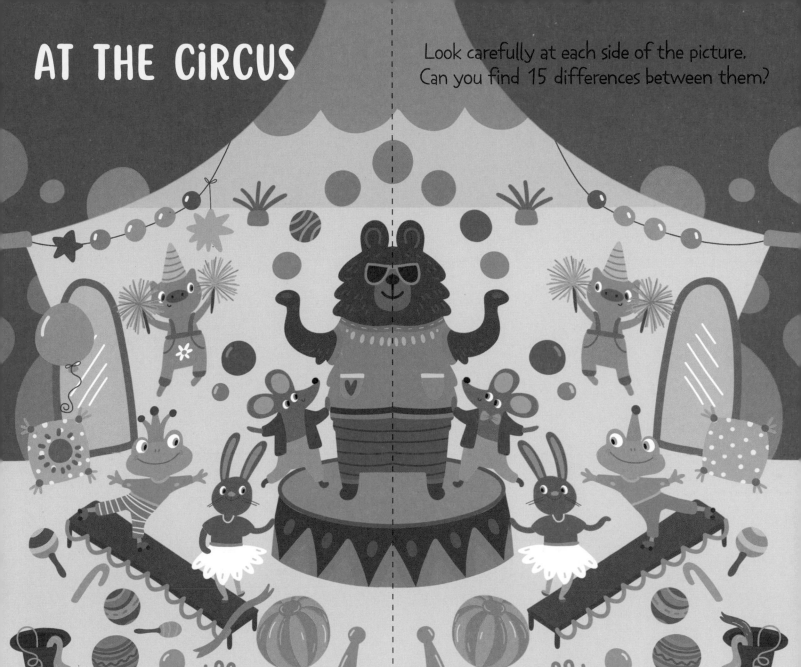

Use your crayons or colored pencils to color
the circus balls.

RUN, MOUSE, RUN!

Jasper is a good hunter, but the mice are fast! Can you help Squeak the mouse get back home safely?

JASPER

SQUEAK

FINISH